Daphney Dollar & Friends

First Trip To The Store

Toys Toys Toys!

Written by Sharon M. Lewis

Illustrated by Mona M. Spencer

Daphney's mom gives her $5 for her allowance and she saves a total of $20. She is so excited about her allowance. She always counts her savings because Daphney wants to buy something special for her daddy's birthday.

As they prepare to go to the mall, Daphney puts her money in her purse and places it in her inner coat pocket, as her mother suggests.

When Daphney enters the mall, she notices a toy store that has a beautiful dancing doll. The doll is on sale for $5. Daphney figures she can spend $5 and still have money to buy her daddy's gift.

When Daphney and her mommy arrive at the Tie Store, they see a whole bunch of ties. Some are plaid, some are polka dots and some are solid colors. Daphney picks the one with the stripes because she knows her daddy likes stripes. When Daphney looks at the price, it is $16.00. Daphney realizes that she does not have enough money to buy the tie. She only has $15 left.

50% Off

$16.00

$5.00

Toys Toys Toys!

That means, the price is actually $8 instead of $16 because half of $16 equals $8.

50% Off

$$16 \div 2 = 8$$

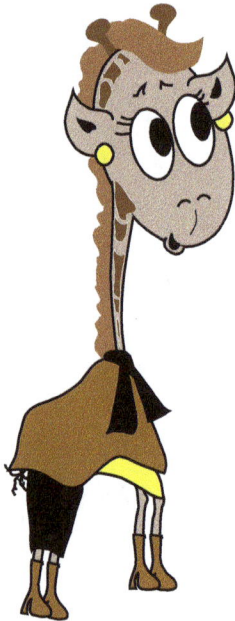

Daddy likes new ties for his birthday.

That's' right, Daphney , daddy surely enjoys his gifts. Now you can purchase the tie so that we can wrap it up for daddy.

Daphney pays for the tie and when she arrives home, she puts the rest of the money in her piggy bank. With her savings, Daphney purchases a doll and a gift for her dad. She even has money left over! Daphney realizes that you can accomplish a goal with careful planning.

Daphney wraps the gift and gives it to her Dad. He is happy that his baby girl saves her allowance. He takes off his old tie and puts on the new tie. He is happy as Daphney imagines he would be.

The End

www.ingramcontent.com/pod-product-compliance
Lightning Source LLC
Chambersburg PA
CBHW050633150426
42811CB00052B/786